Ferenc Juhász

Also by Ferenc Juhász in English

Boy Changed into a Stag: Selected Poems, 1949–67
    (translated by K. McRobbie & J. Ducynska. Oxford University Press, 1970)

Also by David Wevill

Penguin Modern Poets 4 (with David Holbrook & Christopher Middleton, Penguin Books, 1963)
Birth of a Shark (Macmillan / St. Martin's Press, 1964)
A Christ of the Ice-Floes (Macmillan / St. Martin's Press, 1966; Tavern Books, 2016)
Firebreak (Macmillan / St. Martin's Press, 1971)
Where the Arrow Falls (Macmillan, 1973; St. Martin's Press, 1974; Tavern Books, 2016)
Casual Ties (Curbstone, 1983; Tavern Books, 2010; Shearsman Books, 2022)
Other Names for the Heart: New & Selected Poems 1964–1984 (Exile Editions, 1985)
Figure of Eight: New Poems and Selected Translations (Exile Editions, 1987)
Figure of Eight (chapbook; Shearsman Books, 1988)
Child Eating Snow (Exile Editions, 1994)
Solo With Grazing Deer (Exile Editions, 2001)
Departures: Selected Poems (Shearsman Books, 2003; 2013)
Asterisks (Exile Editions, 2007)
To Build My Shadow a Fire: The Poetry and Translations of David Wevill
    (edited by Michael McGriff, Truman State University Press, 2010)
Collected Earlier Poems (Shearsman Books, 2022)
Collected Later Poems (Shearsman Books, 2022)

As translator:
Selected Poems of Ferenc Juhász (with *Selected Poems of Sándor Weöres*, translated
    by Edwin Morgan, Penguin Books, 1970)
Collected Translations (Tavern Books, 2014)
Translations (Shearsman Books, 2022)

Ferenc Juhász

Selected Poems

translated from Hungarian by
David Wevill

Shearsman Books

Published in the United Kingdom in 2022 by
Shearsman Books
P O Box 4239
Swindon
SN3 9FN

Shearsman Books Ltd Registered Office
30–31 St. James Place, Mangotsfield, Bristol BS16 9JB
(this address not for correspondence)

www.shearsman.com

ISBN 978-1-84861-834-3

Translations copyright © David Wevill, 1970, 2022.
The right of David Wevill to be identified as the translator of this work has
been asserted by him in accordance with the
Copyrights, Designs and Patents Act of 1988.
All rights reserved.

Acknowledgments

These translations were first published by Penguin Books in the Penguin Modern European Poets series as half of the volume, Sándor Weöres and Ferenc Juhász, *Selected Poems*, in 1970. A selection was later reprinted in David Wevill, *New Poems and Selected Translations* (Toronto: Exile Editions, 1987), and all were reprinted in David Wevill, *Collected Translations* (Portland, OR: Tavern Books, 2014).

Biographical data on the cover is based on information published in *Hungarian Review*, Budapest.

We are grateful to Dr Katalin Kilián, widow of Ferenc Juhász, for her kind permission to reprint the work contained in this volume.

Contents

Introduction by David Wevill / 9

Part 1

Silver / 17
Gold / 18
Birth of the Foal / 19
Then There Are Fish / 21
Comet-Watchers / 22
Mary / 24
The Tower of Rezi / 25
November Elegy / 28

Part 2

The Boy Changed into a Stag
Clamours at the Gate of Secrets / 33

Part 3

Hunger and Hate / 49
Four Seasons / 50
The Flower of Silence / 52
A Church in Bulgaria / 53
A Message Too Late / 57
Black Peacock / 58
The Rainbow-Coloured Whale / 60
Thursday, Day of Superstition / 65

About the Translator / 73

Introduction

Ferenc Juhász was born 1928, in the village of Bia in western Hungary. His family were peasants. He grew up as part of this peasant community of village and farm, and moved to Budapest in 1945. There he studied art and began writing poetry. His earliest collections, published in 1949 and 1950, won him much prestige and the important Kossuth Prize. To many at this time, Juhász seemed to embody the spirit of Petőfi, the great nineteenth-century poet of Hungary: the same sweeping, epic talent, an awareness of the aspirations of the Hungarian people. But as events changed in Hungary and in Juhász's personal life, the poems became more intense, more self-involved: a dialogue between the poet and the wilderness he filled with prehistoric creatures, proliferating flowers, mythical birds, and a sense of disconnection, bewilderment, strain. "In the years 1957–58 I could not work. Many questions troubled me, besides I was ill for a long time. I thought, I have to begin everything again … even the language has to be made new."

Juhász has written more than any Hungarian poet of his time. His poetry is uneven, and his energy is colossal. His poetry comes from the grass-roots of Hungary: the peasant traditions of folktale and ballad, superstitions, the cycle of life and death. He has a child's eye for nature; a mare with her newborn foal:

And the foal slept at her side,
a heap of feathers ripped from a bed.
Straw never spread as soft as this.
Milk or snow never slept like a foal.

And in 'Comet-Watchers' he describes how the entire village rushes out to watch the phenomenon in the sky:

Over the hill, the star-freaked sky
blazed brighter than burning hay –

> a stallion with wings and a diamond mane,
> a mane of fire, a streaming tail of blood.

There is an affinity between Juhász and Marc Chagall, a "natural wonder." But a poet's world is not so hermetic as a painter's, and as Juhász begins more and more to look around him, his poetry becomes darker. On a visit to a church in Batak, where 4,000 Bulgarians were slaughtered by the Turks nearly a hundred years ago, he is reminded of man's struggle against oppression, and asks:

> What happened here? What does this crying emblem
> mean, here in the heart of the church this once-
> soul and marrow-gifted crown?
> It mourns the madness of power, greed, pride – and the dignity
> of defiance, passion of man and woman,
> for you, you earth, the fiery unquenchable core in us
>   Liberty!

The poem, with its refrain "bone, vertebra, skull,' is a cry against violence and tyranny, and is Juhász's own cry of defiance, his attempt to state his role as a poet. The poem is written at white heat, condemning the "human pig-killing,' the "blood-guzzling" that could happen again if people let it and the exalted sanctuary of the mind, the church, become a "stone coffin."

> Bones, vertebrae, skulls … enough.
> Can my senses still live with this sight,
> this heaped imagery of horror?
> Is there one cell left in my body
> which hasn't suffered the death these bones did?
>
> Is there a cell in my brain
> that isn't part of this grandeur now?
> Have you an ounce of shame left,
> poet? Shame for yourself

> as you stand here, in a white shirt, a summer suit,
> on the stones of this church in August '52?

This poem, 'A Church in Bulgaria', was a declaration and turning point for Juhász. Not overtly a political poet, involved in his own imaginary world, his poems nevertheless begin to reflect his own mood and the mood of the country, as he feels it, more and more. Following Bartók and Zoltán Kodály, he goes back to the ballads and folklore of Hungary, to a deeper vision of Hungary, away from the apparent futility of the present, the emptiness he writes of in 'November Elegy' –

> My mind hunts in circles, sober, ruthless and cold.
> The dull tapping of autumn rain numbs the soul…

where he talks about his "stunted dreams" of "revolutions not fought;' and is reminded of his isolation, his sleeplessness –

> …And even if
> sleep comes, will tomorrow waken anything?

In this poem, and in 'The Seasons', a personal lament written during his wife's illness, there is despair. But the fertility, the noticing things, the involvement with man, animal and flower, is still there. Juhász's fertility often leads to chaos. Many of his poems are wild, organic growths that get out of hand. No detail escapes his attention. What the gardener plants he becomes part of, gets carried away with. But from this nexus have come some remarkable poems.

The greatest of these, perhaps, is 'The Boy Changed into a Stag Clamours at the Gate of Secrets.' The poem is a long allegory whose form and theme have roots in Hungarian folklore, although it is an entirely original creation. It is a poem of two voices. The mother, alone in her old age, calls out to her son to return, tries to lure him back with pleas and motherly promises. But the son has been turned into a stag: he can't return now; if he did, he would destroy her and desecrate his father's grave. Their voices arc back and forth across the poem, calling, answering each other. The mother's world is the home, the stag's world is the forest: the forest of the past and the technological "stone forest" of the future. He stands "on the crest of all time;' at the "gate of secrets;' from which there's no turning back except in death, where he and his mother will be joined:

> you can lay me out in my childhood home,
> with your age-veined hands you can wash my body,
> close my eyelids, swollen glands, with kisses.
>   And when the flesh falls off me,
> and the stench it was sweetens to flowers,
>   I'll be a foetus drinking your blood,
> I'll be your little boy again…

'The Stag' has affinities with Bartók, particularly the *Cantata Profana*. 'The structure and rhythms of the poem derive to some extent from the *regös* – lays, the shaman-songs of ancient Hungary, where there is a magical creature called the Sun Stag who resembles the magic lamb in the ballad 'Fair Maid Julia:'

> It carried the sun and moon between its horns,
> It carried the sparkling star on its brow.
> On its two horns were Ay! two fine gold bracelets,
> Ay! at its sides were two fine burning candles,
> As many as its hairs, so many the stars upon it…

who in turn resembles the stag in Juhász's poem:

> Each branch of my horns
> is a coil of gold rings
> each twig of each branch
> is a candlestick cluster
> each fang-sharp tip
> is a fine funeral candle…

which, as the poem develops, becomes:

> each prong of my antlers a twin-legged pylon
> each branch of my antlers a high-tension wire…

'The Stag' is the finest example of Juhász's use of folk tradition and ballads to create an original allegory that is both personal and universal. It is a total creation that carries all its levels of meaning along with it: the past to which one can never return, but to which one must return in order to find meaning in the present and strength to go beyond. It is where Juhász cuts himself adrift from the powers and certainties he relied on in the past. Like the poem 'Rainbow-Colored Whale', addressed to the grave of his father, it is a summation and farewell:

> Life here is peaceful
> without you.
> Flower then, flower into
> the death-wish of the lily.

Juhász is a poet at odds with his time. His weapons are not irony, allusion or insinuation, but energy, imagination, and a passionate "Hungarian-ness" that he gets from his peasant background. His poetry shows very little literary influence, none of the fashions or styles of the time: he is a native product, touched by surrealism perhaps, whose real roots are in the ballads and folksongs of Hungary. His own vision of Hungary, with which he identifies himself, isolates him from the "huge merry-go-round" of the neon world he sees developing around him where, in the city on a rainy night, he sees the "neon monsters" the beasts of the past return:

> A bestiary
> of red, blue, green and yellow faces…

– a world where man walks alone, where it is "not permitted" to cry out or complain:

> Where am I going?
> What song am I singing?

Juhász is disillusioned with man's ability to accept substitutes, the artificial – to accept them until reality comes, unrecognised, and destroys him. He has tried to create his own mythology, to express an elemental vision, a totality however chaotic, to set against the world of statistics, paper forms and evasions. His enormous body of poetry is uneven. But he's written some of the finest poems of his time. Speaking out for himself and, one feels, for Hungary, he ends this last poem, 'Thursday, Day of Superstition':

> Hell-bent on life, like a sponge, I head for home
> in the red, green and blue rain: in the age of socialism.

This selection of Juhász's poems was chosen by Flora Papastavrou and myself. I do not know Hungarian, and these translations could not have been done without Mrs. Papastavrou's insight, imagination and enthusiasm. She did the roughs, and unlocked many of the poems for me by her interpretations and suggestions; so it was a joint effort. I would like to thank István Siklós, who read the manuscript, made suggestions, and provided me with notes. And also the National Translation Center, Austin, Texas, whose grant helped me to go on with the work.

D.W. (1970)

Part 1

Silver

The traveller stands in the freezing cold
surrounded by drowsy old men.
His moustache is ice, his eyelashes
inhuman half-moons of silver.
He stands watching the horses,
the snow dusting under their hooves
like a cloud of millions of comets
misting the milky star-roads.
His ears are silver, his hair is silver.
The horses twitch their manes and tails.
Silver the velvet nostrils, the steaming flanks.

Gold

The woman touches her bun
of thinning hair. She laughs,
and drops a spoon and a hunk of bread
in their reaching, grubby hands.
Like roses divining water
the circle of thin red necks
leans over the steaming plates;
red noses bloom in the savoury mist.

The stars of their eyes shine
like ten worlds lost in their own light.
In the soup, slowly circling
swim golden onion rings.

Birth of the Foal

As May was opening the rosebuds,
elder and lilac beginning to bloom,
it was time for the mare to foal.
She'd rest herself, or hobble lazily

after the boy who sang as he led her
to pasture, wading through the meadowflowers.
They wandered back at dusk, bone-tired,
the moon perched on a blue shoulder of sky.

Then the mare lay down,
sweating and trembling, on her straw in the stable.
The drowsy, heavy-bellied cows
surrounded her, waiting, watching, snuffing.

Later, when even the hay slept
and the shaft of the Plough pointed south,
the foal was born. Hours the mare
spent licking the foal with its glue-blind eyes.

And the foal slept at her side,
a heap of feathers ripped from a bed.
Straw never spread as soft as this.
Milk or snow never slept like a foal.

Dawn bounced up in a bright red hat,
waved at the world and skipped away.
Up staggered the foal,
its hooves were jelly-knots of foam.

Then day sniffed with its blue nose
through the open stable window, and found them –
the foal nuzzling its mother,
velvet fumbling for her milk.

Then all the trees were talking at once,
chickens scrabbled in the yard,
like golden flowers
envy withered the last stars.

Then There Are Fish

Forever confusing smoke with weeds,
clouds and sky with water.

Born with no lungs, just a blister
floating in a cage of splinters,
listless fins and hyperthyroid eyes.

Even the smallest fry
chase their hunger as boldly as carp –
mouths, nostrils, eyes
burst on a rising scream like a shoal of bubbles.

A world of nothing but water!

Houses and trees
float up like giant bubbles.

Comet-Watchers

One blind-calm summer night
someone tapped at the window of our house –
"Come out! Come out!
There's a miracle! There, in the sky!"

We jumped out of bed. What is it?
some secret message from the stars?
I grabbed my mother's hand, it was warm,
I felt her heart beat in my palm.

Barefooted, in shirts and underpants
the whole village gathered out there in the cold;
scared old women, sleep-white faces
frozen in the white light of another world.

The poor came crowding into the street.
Women crossed their arms over their breasts.
Their knees shook as they gaped at the sky –
a fairytale, a holy prophecy!

Over the hill, the star-freaked sky
blazed brighter than burning hay –
a stallion with wings and a diamond mane,
a mane of fire, a streaming tail of blood.

I gripped my mother's hand like roots.
I remember the warmth of her body still,
and father pointing up at the horse
blazing away in the fires of its own sweat.

Proudly it flew away over the roofs.
We stood, still as gravestones in its fierce light.
The sky was much darker when it had gone.
O fate of comets, will o' the wisp, our hope!

Mary

Like a little cow swollen with calf
she moons around the field, cow-eyed and staring.
The moon's silver belly hangs low in the sky,
the moon beginning to ebb, and the seas
ebbing with the moon.
She remembers the horde of children
locked in their room, shouting, their faces
pushed between the window-bars,
heads poking out to spy on the world,
red eyelids, petals of blood-red rose.
She loiters slowly away
like a little cow swollen with calf,
her rump swaying as she ambles along.
Above her the stars shine hard and cold.
Her heartbeats are too loud…
she doesn't understand … she stops,
looks down at her belly, and feels
the little feet kicking like a heart.

The Tower of Rezi

I sit here in the Rezi tower
under a massing of swallows –
through my field glasses I follow
their soaring, darting flight.

Below me the yellow harvest land,
poplars and mown fields;
the old forests shedding their leaves,
mist melting distance.

My eyes are glassy stalks,
they catch a swallow as it dips.
It is held in the glasses' lens,
trapped, in a fairytale glass tower.

The wonder of this magic spell –
modern wizardry!
It flies so near it's as if
its wings would flit through my pupils.

Inside me now: it dips and dives,
curves, wheels, flutters, drops
(through my body) so lightly,
drunker and drunker with the wind.

I can feel the flutter of lungs,
the ounce of heart's motor –
rib cage, feather, tail –
lawgivers of the flight's arc.

And I'm flying – it's me, not the bird!
The wonders this lens can do!
The self swirling and dipping
forgets it is only watching.

I'm a spiralling, tiny
swallow now. O you swallows!
I'm hurried aloft and held in the arms
of endless space.

My heart has become a bird,
put on feathers, grown wings –
I share
the soaring infinity of the bird.

Most wonderful, wonderful flight!
Joy, pain, sweetness, tears.
The circling heart feels no boundaries,
each curve brings it nearer to heaven.

And I know, what traps it too
is the huge eye of the lens
(for it wants to escape) – already
its beak makes signals of distress.

Then suddenly, in a careless moment
it breaks from the path of the lens –
swallow, where are you? Heart?
Torn clean away with the rest of the swallow-flock.

Through the field glasses I search
blue nothingness.
Nothing but the infinite there.
What happened? Am I left with no heart?

November Elegy

My mind hunts in circles, sober, ruthless and cold.
The dull tapping of autumn rain numbs the soul.
Rain drips from the ivy leaves
in heavy, sticky threads: earth, sky, the roof-eaves
sweat with fever. Soon there'll be nothing alive!
I can't sleep, my mind has lost its wings.
My brain is a live coal, the bedclothes are flames
eating my bones. Ships' horns
cry from the Danube. The light from the street is sick,
it throws ghostly leaves on the wall, and tricks
the still, painted horses in my friend's
picture – whinnying, they dance from their frame.
I put my arm around you, your touch soothes me.
Under my hand your breathing is poetry,
pulse, rhythm, ebb, flow, the heart's knocking.
But sleep won't come, the rhythm's lame, and shies away –
the clear voice of sleep can't sing
my stunted dreams: of revolutions not fought,
memories, fevers, desires that swirl in the heart's
bottomless slush, churned by the killer hooves of contradictions.
My soul steams and smells like vegetation
after a sulphurous summer night of storms.
I get up, stand at the window: hollow, echoing sounds
from the town below, a baby's cry, an animal wailing.
Nightsmoke lies in the trees, reminding
me I am alone, how alone.
That sound I heard was the last tram flashing home
over the bridge, writing its sign in the rain.
And now, like someone slowly crossing the room,

a scythe taps on the wall ... hallucinations!
I must lie down and rest. Sleep, so the nerves and brain
can heal. And the heart, the idiot heart.
My eyes burn, I can't sleep. And even if
sleep comes, will tomorrow waken anything?

Part 2

The Boy Changed into a Stag
Clamours at the Gate of Secrets

The mother called to her own son,
cried from far away,
the mother called to her own son,
cried from far away,
went to the front of the house: from there she cried,
unwound her heavy knot of hair
dusk wove to a shimmering bride's veil
that flowed down to her ankles
a flag, tasselled, black, for the wind
the firedamp dusk that smelled of blood.
She knotted her fingers to tendrils of stars,
the moon-froth covered her face,
and like this she cried to her dear son
as once she'd cried to her child –
stood in front of the house and spoke to the wind
spoke to the songbirds
to the love-cries of the wild geese
shouted across to the wind-fingered reeds
to the luminous sprawled potato-flower
to the stocky, cluster-balled bulls
to the sumac tree, shade of the well,
she called to the jumping fish
to the welding rings of water –

    Hush! you birds and branches
hush, because I'm calling
    be still, fishes and flowers
be still, I want to speak

    be quiet, breath of the soil
    fin-quiver, leafy parasols
be still, deep humming of sap
rumours that seep from the atoms' depths
    bronze-chaste virgins, wool-breasted flock
be quiet, because I'm calling,
I'm crying out to my own son!

    The mother called to her own son,
    the scream rose upward, writhing
    spiralling in the vortex of the universe –
    its blade glittered in the light
    like the scales of a spinning fish,
    like metal in roads, nitre in caves.
    The mother called to her own son:
come back, my dear son, come back
I am calling you, I, your own mother!
I am calling you, I, your riverbed
    I am calling you, your fountainhead
come back, my son, come back
    I call you, your memory's teat
come back, my son, come back
    I call you, your ragged tent
come back, my son, come back
    I call you, your guttering lamp.

Come back my son, I'm always knocking against things,
I have bruise-stains under my eyes, on the skin of my brow,
my calves, my thighs –
objects charge and butt me like angry rams,
the garden stake, chairs, the fence, gore me terribly,
doors thump me like Saturday drunkards,
the light's broken, the switch gives me shocks,

blood crawls in the skin of veins as through the beak of a stone-
                                                    bruised bird,
    the scissors swim off like metal crabs,
matchsticks hop like sparrows' legs, the bucket handle hits back –
come back, my dear son, come back
I can no longer run like the young mother doe,
    my legs are ripe with bindweed,
    knotty, purplish roots grow in my thighs,
my toes swell with calcium-mounds,
    my fingers stiffen, with flesh tough as shell,
like snail's horn, scaly, like old shale-rock,
    my branches are sickly, dry and ready to snap –
come back, my son, come back
    for I'm spellbound,
    haggard, and full of visions –
    they flicker from my decaying glands
    as winter morning cock-crow
pings off the frozen shirts hung on a fence –
I call you, your own mother
come back, my son, come back –
give meaning to all these things,
control them again: tame the knife,
    make the stubborn comb show itself,
for I'm just two green gritty eyes,
bubbles of light: like a dragonfly,
    which as you know, my child
    carries between its nape and jaw
two crystal apples that fill its whole skull,
I am two huge eyes without a face,
and their vision is not of this world.
Come back, my son, come back –
    breathe life into things again.

The boy listened,
he tossed his head,
with nostrils like pails he
sniffed, his dewlap quivering –
his veined ears pricked at the sound
of that crying voice, his body tensed
as if sensing the hunter's footstep
or a whiff of smoke in the forest
when the smoke-blue forest
mourns its own burning, whimpering.
He swung his head that way
hearing the familiar voice cry,
suddenly stiffened with fear –
on his rump he noticed the fur,
discovered the split hooves,
stared at his cudweed shanks,
at his furry buck-apples
hidden there, where the lily shines.
He galloped across to a pool,
his chest ploughed through ferns,
body a muck of foam,
gouts of lather smacking the ground;
his four black hooves
stamp life from the flowers,
a tiny lizard is squashed, its
crushed neck-bib and tail grow cold.
He stoops over the pool,
stares into the moonlit water –
a beech tree with the moon in its hair
shudders – the pool reflects a stag!
Then he sees that the thick fur
covers his body all over –
fur covers his knees and thighs,

his tassel-lipped penis sheath,
and antlers grow from his head
where the bone-branches had budded,
his face is furred to the chin,
the cut of his nostrils slanting in.
He whacks his antlers against a tree,
his neck a rope of veins,
paws the ground, the nerves strain
choking to bellow a cry –
but it's only the voice of a stag
his mother hears echoing back –
he'd weep the tears of a son,
and blows till the watery monster is gone,
blows, and in his breath's whirlpool
in the liquid midnight sparkle
little fishes with petal fins
scatter, their eyes like diamond-bubbles.
When the water's feathers settle again
it is a stag that stands in the moon-foam.

Now the boy shouted back
    bellowing, stretching his neck
the boy shouted back
    a stag's voice wildering through the fog –
mother, mother
I can't go back
mother, my mother
don't call me back
my nurse, my nurture
mother, mother
marvellous foaming spring
roof I grew up under
breasts with swollen buds

tent sheltering me from the frost
mother, my mother
don't ask me to come
mother, my mother
my one silky flower
my bird of gold
mother, mother
don't call me back!
If I were to go back
my antlers would spear you,
my horns: tip to tip
I'd toss your old body –
if I were to go back
I'd tumble you on the ground
with these hooves I'd squash
your little breasts
my horns would stab you and stab
you, I'd bite you –
I'd trample your loins
if I went back
mother, mother
I'd rip you soul from body
bluebottles would flock to it –
the stars would gape
in shame at your soft lily-cleft,
though this gave me once
such lovely, tender warmth
in its lustre of oils,
warmth such as the breathing
cattle gave Jesus.
Mother, mother
you mustn't call me –
you'd turn to stone

you'd die, if you saw
your son coming.
Each branch of my horns
is a coil of gold rings
each twig of each branch
is a candlestick-cluster
each fang-sharp tip
is a fine funeral candle
each lace frond of horn
is a gold altar-cloth.
Believe me, you'd die
if you saw my sprawling
antlers filling the sky –
as on All Souls' Eve
the graveyard is lit
by candles, leaf by leaf,
my head is a petrified tree.
Mother, mother
if I found you
I'd scorch you to
a blackened stump,
I'd burn you to a lump
of greasy clay,
I'd roast you to chunks
of charred black meat.
Mother, mother
don't call to me –
if I went back
I'd eat you up
I'd wreck the house
with my thousand-tipped horns
I'd slash
the flowerbeds to pieces

I'd rip up the trees
with my stag's teeth
I'd swallow the well
in one gulp –
if I went back
I'd set fire to the house
then I'd gallop off
to the burial plot
and with delicate nose
and all four hooves
I'd dig up my father –
I'd tear off the lid
of his coffin with my teeth –
I'd scatter his bones!
Mother, mother
don't call me back,
I can't go back.
If I did go back,
I would kill you.

So the boy cried with a stag's voice,
and the mother answered him,
    come back, come back my son
I'm calling you, I, your own mother
    come back, my son, come back
I'll cook you sour-cabbage soup, you can slice onion-rings into it,
they'll crunch in your teeth like bits of stone in a giant's jaws,
I'll give you warm milk in a clean glass,
in my cellar the lair of fire-bellied frogs
in my cellar blinking like a giant green toad
I'll gently pour wine into heron-necked bottles,
with my stony fists I'll knead bread – for I know, I know

how to bake round little froth-bellied loaves, and Sunday twists –
    come back, come back my son
I plucked the crops of live, shrieking geese for your featherbed,
I cried I plucked the geese cried … the feather-wounds drooled white fat,
I sunned your straw mattress, I shook it out,
the clean-swept courtyard is listening for you, the table is laid.
    Aiii mother, mother
        I cannot go back,
don't give me your twists of milk-loaf
    or sweet goat's milk in a flowered glass
Don't make my bed springy and soft
    or pluck out the throats of the geese –
throw the wine away, pour it over your father's grave
    weave the onions into a wreath,
fry your frothy doughnuts for the little ones now.
    For the warm milk would turn to vinegar in my mouth,
    a stone would squat in place of the milk loaf,
    the wine in my glass would turn to blood,
    each soft bed-feather become a flame,
    the small drinking mug a blade of blue sword-lily.
Aiii mother, aiii, aiii mother –
    I can't go back to my birthplace now.
Only the green forest can hold me,
    the house is too small for my huge, furry horns,
the courtyard has no space for my graveyard antlers,
    the shaking world-tree of my branching antlers
with stars as its leaves, the Milky Way as its moss.
    I can only eat sweet-smelling grass,
the tender young grass is my cud –
    I can no longer drink from a flowered glass,
only from a spring, only from a clean, fresh spring!

I don't understand, I don't understand your strange talk, son
you speak with a stag's voice, the soul of a stag moves in you, my poor one.
When the turtledove weeps, turtledove weeps, the little bird calls,
                            little bird calls, my son
why am I, why am I in all creation the unhappy one?
Do you still remember, still remember your little mother, my son?
I don't understand, I don't understand your piteous crying, son.
Do you remember how happily you'd come running home, with your
                            school-report,
you dissected frogs, nailed their speckled webby hands to the fence,
lost yourself in your airplane books, helped me in with the washing?
You were in love with Irena B – V.J., and H.S. the painter, his beard
                            like a wild orchid, was your friend.
Do you remember, Saturday nights when your father came home
                            sober, how happy you were?
Aiii, mother, mother, don't remind me. My sweetheart and friends,
   they swam from me cold like fish. The poppy-throated painter,
   who knows where he went, mother – where my youth went?
Mother, mother don't mention my father. Sorrow flowers, blossoms
                          from his flesh of earth. Don't
                          mention my father –
   he'll get up from his grave, gather up his yellow bones
   and come staggering out-his nails, his hair sprouting again.
Aiii, aiii! Old Wilhelm came, the coffin maker, runt with a doll's face.
   He said, I'll grab your feet, we'll put you nicely into the box –
   but I started retching with fear. I'd just come back from Pest,
   you used to go there too, by train … a caretaker … the rails got
                          twisted
   Aiii, I'd have to cut myself to pieces, the candle puddling shadows
                          on your taut face –
Latzi, our new brother-in-law, the barber, shaved you. The candles
                          drooled like babies,

  their innards melting out, dribbles, the bowels gleaming, the nerves
         shining through.
The Choral Society stood around in their purple caps, lowing your
         death like cattle,
and I touched your forehead. Your hair was alive,
I heard it grow, saw the bristles beginning on your chin –
by morning your chin was black, next day your throat was spiky
        like stalks of viper's bugloss,
a slice of hairy melon, a yellow caterpillar with a blue-cabbage skin.
Aiii, I thought it would outgrow the room, the courtyard, the whole world
  your beard and hair, the stars in it humming like vermin.
Aiii, aiii ! In the dense green of rain, the red horses pulling your hearse
         whinnied in fear –
one kicked out at your head, the other pissed helplessly, its purple
sex flopped out like a hanged man's tongue, the coachman swore,
rain washed the blare of the brass band, your mates were blowing
         and sobbing,
stood blowing by the thorny, thistled chapel wall,
blew out a basket of silvery breath from their puffed black lips,
blew the tune with cracked bloody lips and bloodshot eyes,
blew the card games, wines-and-sodas, the bloated and withered women,
blew the minted planets of coins, baksheesh, up into the void after you,
blew the thick dust of hopelessness away, sobbing. The tune
blared from the hard, glinting, O-mouthed horns into a void stinking
         of corpses –
petrified loves, decaying women, the mouldering militias of grandfathers,
cottages, cradles, enamel and silver onion pocket-watches,
Easter bells multiplying redeemers like a bird's wing fanning,
trumpeting briefcases, train-wheels, brass-buttoned ratings stiff
         with salutes.
They blew with gum-pink teeth, the friends, with black puffy liver lips,
and you led them: That's it, lads! That's great! Aiii, don't stop playing –

your hands, crossed, a pair of golden spiders, long legs, jointed, hinged
                spokes of your heart.
Your shoes in the cupboard wait for the next-of-kin, your bread-
                crust-callous feet look childlike,
      helpless in their white socks,
  and your mates blew on in the dashing rain, the trumpet-stops
              hiccupped like steel adam's apples,
  like claws of the reptile-bird, Carcharodon's teeth, the brass
              trumpets glittered.
Aiii, mother, mother, don't speak of my father.
    Leave him be, his eyes stare from the earth like buds.

The mother called to her own son,
    cried, from far away
come back my son, come back
    come away from that stone world
stag of the stone forest, smogs, electric grids and neon glitter.
    The iron bridges and tramlines, they thirst for your blood,
        a hundred times a day they jab you, but you never hit back –
    I am calling you, I, your own mother
        come back my son, come back.

There he stood on the crest of all time,
there he stood on creation's highest mountain,
there he stood at the gate of secrets –
the points of his antlers played with the stars
and with a stag's voice he cried,
cried back to his mother who'd borne him –
    mother, mother, I can't go back
the hundred wounds in me weep pure gold,
I die every day, a hundred bullets in me
every day I get up again a hundred times stronger
I die every day three billion deaths

and three billion times a day I am born,
each prong of my antlers a twin-legged pylon
each branch of my antlers a high-tension wire,
my eyes are ports of cargo-ships, my veins are greased cables,
my teeth are iron bridges, my heart is a thrashing ocean of monsters,
each vertebra is a thriving city, my spleen is a chuffing stone-barge,
each cell is a vast factory, every atom a solar system,
my testicles are the sun and moon, the Milky Way is my spine-marrow,
each point in space is one grain of my body,
each galaxy an inkling of my brain.

Son, my lost son, I still wane you back –
    your mother's eyes, like a dragonfly's, won't rest until you come.

To die I'll come back, only to die.
To die I'll come back,
mother – only to die will I come.
Then you can lay me out in my childhood home,
with your age-veined hands you can wash my body,
close my eyelids, swollen glands, with kisses.
    And when the flesh falls off me,
and the stench it was sweetens to flowers,
    I'll be a foetus drinking your blood,
I'll be your little boy again –
and this hurts only you, mother,
    aiii, hurts only you, mother.

Part 3

Hunger and Hate

If there were a god I'd deny him.
I'd hammer the dead flesh of his face.
I'd snap at his hand like a dog as he stooped
to pat me. With tears and a gun I'd waylay him.

I'd take a rainbow-quick sliver
of glass, and gouge his balls out.
I'd slash at his groin till the pain
was red-hot and his blood gushed rust like oil.

I'd gnaw at his shinbone
with its spidery hairs, a mad dog
foaming away the obedient centuries –

then I'd yank his heart out, like the shark
biting through all the ages of fish on the hook –
a greasy stomach, a mottled blue fin.

Four Seasons

      Autumn is gone. The leaves have turned to mould.
     I tramped over the mush of planes on my way to you.
    My orphaned eyes skulked in holes the dead had abandoned
  like hermit crabs in the dead shells they crawl to.
   The whale-mouthed iron railings dribbled violet shadows of the dead,
spongy babies, stale chrysanthemums, hung from their lips, moaning
                           and crying.
   They brought me a blue turtledove, a gold chain and a bell on
                        its tiny leg.
I drowned in your atom-splitting smile, your moongaze turned my
                           hair grey.

     And winter's over. Not like winters we knew.
     A sky of bone crackles in the jaws of the church bells.
    Teeth chattering like machine guns I went out begging crumbs for you.
     The still forest glittered like broken glass.
   Shadows blue as hyacinth blurred from the frosted railings,
and grieving, hooded in quiet, the animals, tiptoeing, circled your window.
   By the bed I listened to your breezy chatter, like a jasmine rustling,
and red deer, hare, pheasant, thrush, heard the white flame of
                       your song in the churned snow.

     And now it is spring. A soft mould-flush
      oozes and sticks to the walls in a thin green glaze.
   Dead flower-heads drift and soak in the jelly mush,
and death circles in from the void, misting the eyes.
     The blotchy railings vomit bile-green shadows
where man-eating fish and stars with shark's teeth swirl home to the feast,

brought by sick lusts and stale prayers, mad gibberings and curses.
And I, an elder tree on your dead-alive grave, throw myself on the stelae
of your breasts.

Summer will come, mincing us gold with light.
On the moon the magic unicorn rears with his blue grin.
And the wailing world remembers its griefs, the nerves tensing
around it.
In its ultraviolet scum, the insect breeds to distraction;
acid shadows drip from the peeling railings,
and butterflies burn to ash on your heart, as the lizard's fist squeezes it.
In this garden of ferns I hear your girl-flower weeping.
In this cave of blood-red stones I moan to you, a black leopard buried
alive in your heart.

The Flower of Silence

The flower of silence fades to grief's huge funeral leaves
Don't cry don't scream don't tear me apart with your eyes
Don't tie me to the grieving cross with live ropes weeping blood
I'm drying up my flesh my glands death is a shimmer of flies

My nerve-tentacles weave through the dripping stars
Squeezing and sucking the blood of starfish I'm drunk
I'm a mad green eye whirled on the poles of its grief
Help me my carnivore mask has eaten away my face

Go back to the forest I heard the song of the stag
Silence is every leaf the trees grow noiselessly
Peace is a wandering doe the birds are scarlet flowers
My heart seed of your heart the flower of silence opens.

A Church in Bulgaria

Inside a church in Batak in 1876, 4,000
Bulgarians were massacred by the Turks.

Wreathed into the earth, a stone coffin, this church,
an unbreakable stone bubble:
it wants to flutter away, soar in the air
but is torn by its dead weight down into the soil –
earth gnaws at its solid mass
through the spidery roots which suckle it too.
Like a horse's skull stripped of its glory of flesh,
the past! a grinning skull
which the humus hasn't buried quite –
humus, the earth, the oval cropland
which whirls with us, rolls in the burning dust of space.
And what's kept there, hoarded
deep, as in men's hearts? What's buried there,
dragged down into itself incalculable
millions of years: silence which won't complain?
Bone, vertebra, skull, self-sweat,
metal, coal and fern;
earth's earliest beasts crystallized in unknown layers,
flowers of the far past, fish cut in stone,
old anthems, shards of forgotten epics
and again: bone, vertebra, skull,
whole millennia of flaking eyes,
prehistoric fish-rot, gases, oils,
statues the marble limbs of dead cities
lost in the stale and fresh strata, they jab at the earth from beneath;
and lava, the liquid fire earth spews at will.

This seeps from the earth, earth dries it, like sweat on a thinking head,
or a mammoth brain its own thoughts,
time without end.

Earth I stand on, here, bloodsoaked stones
I won't pry deeper, or ask more of your past.
The lesson is here, in the blood-ruined beams
of this stone skull blown by man's brain, walls clenched under its weight
like old men's shoulders already bending
under, to earth. There they'll fall. Where the stones grew
was man's source too: he was cast up from it
like the fish from water. Above him the dust tides over
unruffled, still: just rolls with a smothering rumble.

For they're here too: bones, vertebrae, skulls, a yellow
heap in the marble coffin's belly of mirrors –
bones, vertebrae, skulls. Look, like a lime-bubble
or water-bead: white bones with a baby's head,
or an old man's, like a black sod,
a tiny shinbone, knotty and yellow and
hollow like a straw; a carious, fat
starshaped vertebra, twisted fingerbones,
a skull drilled with bullet holes
like a maggoty fruit, a virgin's delicate
knotted kneecap, like a walking stick – all one spiky heap
like a hayrick pitched over stakes out on a lake.
For the coffin's reflecting belly of mirrors
flashes one lesson a thousand ways –
bone, vertebra, skull.

What happened here? What does this crying emblem
mean, here in the heart of the church this once –
soul and marrow-gifted crown?

It mourns the madness of power, greed, pride – and the dignity
of defiance, passion of man and woman,
for you, you earth, the fiery unquenchable core in us
    Liberty!

The defiance whose eyes would drill through rock
rather than smile for dictators.
Man's stubbornness is such
he'd sooner gnash his tongue to a bloody
spittle than thank his oppressors.
And the courage: woman who'd show her full white breasts
like the Carpathian heights under snow,
as a mocking gift to the knives christian or
infidel – but cries "Be damned to you, murderer!"
And the honour, this hairy male-breast
more muscular than the chest of a horse, he
bares to their guns, steel weaker than his gaze.

Here the blood rose high as their heads, trembling –
dome and window moist with its ruby steam,
in this church, the eye of a dragonfly husk.
Here it stood, a black jelly of fear,
the slaughtered patriots' blood –
men, women and children who stood
silently frowning, victims watching
this blood-rampage of power.
For the human heart endures much
but can't live in its iron bands forever –
suddenly it flares up like a dying star,
anger gushing energy in a shower of fire.
Which is what these did: the downtrodden
raised their arms and eyes against the oppressor.

O he knew already the game was over,
the trick lost, the dice gone dead in his hand!
So before he'd crouch terrified over the horse's mane
and escape on the stallion flying with swollen nostrils and veins
sweating crimson froth, he held,
here, a last feast, a human pig-killing.
For still he craved flesh, lusted to be drunk
on the steaming crimson broth, that magic stallion.
Drop by drop he filled the stone communion cup with blood.
This blood-guzzling, this stony eucharist, is history now.

The seared village, fired huts,
virgins spitted on swords, women
with marble skins ripped by diamond spear-holes,
broken lilies, gouged eyes
weeping like squashed plums –
these visions, like the mica-flakes of the Milky Way
remain, to haunt the child of a later century.
As here, now: the bones, vertebrae, skulls, heaped up
holy reminder and lesson,
in this church shocked to stone.
Bones, vertebrae, skulls … enough.
Can my senses still live with this sight,
this heaped imagery of horror?
Is there one cell left in my body
which hasn't suffered the death these bones did?

Is there a cell in my brain
that isn't part of this grandeur now?
Have you an ounce of shame left,
poet? Shame for yourself
as you stand here, in a white shirt, a summer suit,
on the stones of this church in August '52?

A Message Too Late

I read your poems again, my friend.
I read them slowly, line by line,
thumbing the pages, thinking of you, my friend.
And why deny it? I wept at the thought of your name.
I wasn't sorting them, sheep from goats
like a mustering of autumn conscripts –
I just gave up and stared at the massed rows
of your poems, your whole identity, friend.
Here your dry X-ray sight opens
the cave-dwellers' lair, and the flowers of doubt,
and the wings of the pterodactyl, flesh-eater, bird-father,
to get at the secrets of the human heart.
Like the surgeon in Rembrandt's picture
you showed us dissection, you raped a dead world's nerves.
How you must have sweated days,
bringing those nightmare facts to life!
Hunched over the corpse's rainbow guts
by the light of the smelly oil lamp in your cellar,
your dry obsession made your fingers itch –
but in the end, what can a corpse tell you?
Well it's here, we see it. You forced us to see.
Now what will cleanse the infection from our eyes?
You never forgave us our wrongheadedness –
but is there no hope? Not one refreshing word?
Just one word as clear as the rain
that gives birth to a homeland or curses a world?

Black Peacock

Points, angles, hollows, lines, all
meet in this head: rough-chiselled, its veins still showing.
The eye is ringed with a deep
moat of sadness, a trench hammered out of tin.

Remember, Pishta, the winter nights would cry –
"Even Jesus shouldered his own green tree!
Someone's kissing Pishta's girl, and it isn't he!"

Lurching like an old gravestone,
he rubs against the nudging shoulders of women.
His tears are knives with mother-of-pearl handles.
His words kindle timeless shivers under their skin.

Pishta, old friend, remember when we sat
on the Danube embankment, on top of that marble post,
and love wailed and cried like something lost.

He has no father or mother.
Perhaps God dreamed him up
to ease his own conscience. But when he turns
to dust the Phoenix is born, the snowdrop opens.

Remember, Pishta, remember
the sky was a wireless bringing us news, it was winter,
we wept: can one still kiss and play the lover?

On his heart a black peacock struts and cries.
Talk to him … he lurches away, won't answer.
Won't talk, but listens for the peacock step.
Does nothing but cry, in the spell of the peacock's cry.

Remember, Pishta, old friend of mine,
those days when love was like a bottle of wine,
a moonlit track cutting through snow and pine.

Girls, don't tear him to pieces
like convicts squabbling over a loaf of bread.
Griefs, don't rant and scrabble around him
like furies over the heart of a dying man.

Pishta, remember the other day
I swore I would let myself waste away
if I didn't find my life's share of joy?

Now those who can love, and kill for love,
have time enough to hate him,
if from this bundle of points, angles, hollows
and lines, only silence, numbness, is left of him.

The Rainbow-Coloured Whale

Now your grave is sinking,
like your back
when the scalpel
cut away your ribs.

They say, the wreath
we laid at your head has withered,
the plank's gone rotten
that propped your dead heart.

Your grave is sinking deeper,
a black mouth lying in wait.
Every day I bring fresh earth
in a big willow basket.

But the earth I bring in the evening
is gone by morning;
the earth I bring in the morning
by nightfall has sunk without trace.

As if you were eating
and eating your way through the earth,
forever upwards,
with those toothless gums.

The salt-spray eating the coral
becomes the coral –
the worm devoured you,
now you devour the worm.

You eat through it all
like a huge grub,
insatiable mouth without stomach,
munching into daylight.

Tons of stones and clay –
nothing can stop those jaws!
What can you want in our world
with your dead will?

Skull, Nothing,
what is it you want?
Learn the final lesson.
You are alone now.

Rainbow-colored whale,
swimming the waters under the earth,
obey the laws of the earth,
the vows of death and burial.

Earth swallowed you whole,
and you swallowed the whole world.
No hope, no body left –
it's time you understood.

Rainbow-coloured whale, thrashing and
churning the clogged waters under the earth,
you are a predator now,
not worthy of what you were.

When you were alive your skin
was a breathing marsh of colours,
your sweat gushed in little
squirts, like hypodermics.

But you haven't noticed
how naked you've grown,
how the black earth
has melted you.

Those cold eyes that knew
the stone-green world of boulder and pine
have burst by now,
soft, like seaweed pods.

You didn't even know
they'd betrayed you –
sold every ounce of you
for Judas-gold!

The traces left in the air
by your wandering desires –
gone forever,
under the hoarfrost.

And whatever sediment remained
of your heart
has been turned to stone,
melted away with the waters.

Little by little
time has eaten
the tartar from your teeth,
the grief from your eyes.

And it's time you learnt
not to see hope in such signs.
When a man dies,
he loses his will to live.

My grief for you was like thorns,
but the thorns have withered.
The green tree of your absence
is slowly beginning to flower.

The tusks of the black boar,
the tusks of the black boar that
slashed you open –
the sting has gone out of the wound.

But why were you never
as hungry as this –
so hungry I feel you
unwinding out of the grave?

No man has the right
to live it all over again!
I haven't the strength
to bury you twice!

Look, your sea's dried up –
don't thrash about
in the earth's black surf
as if it were water.

You'd swallow the sun
like a goldfish?
Strain the sumac tree
through your teeth, like parsley?

Bone-flower,
burrowing towards the light,
don't ever blossom. Don't gnaw
into our moonlight with your rat's teeth.

Larva,
don't eat your way into my heart.
I live with your absence.
You don't exist.

Life here is peaceful
without you.
Flower then, flower into
the death-wish of the lily.

Thursday, Day of Superstition

On the third day it is hardest, on the third.

Distracted, nowhere to go,
I roam this island of stone and neon, the Octagon.
It is Thursday evening,
no time for cursing,
no time for crying.

Red, blue, yellow, green, the rain is falling.
The streets are rainbows
riddled with pattering bubbles.
The bubble-creatures roll their eyes
like chameleons, round and round
as a pebble rolls in a clay jar.
Their watery skins
ripple from colour to colour –
the lizards of rain crawl all over each other.
This island is Galápagos,
this lonely flowering of stones.

I am alone.

The island spins like a huge merry-go-round.
Taxis, buses, trams – step up for the joy-ride!
The shop-fronts whirl round and round like drunken stars.
The sword-lilies are whores in this amusement park.

Red, blue, yellow, green, the rain is falling.
The news-vendors are shouting.
The flower-sellers say nothing.

To the rooftops, silent, glowing,
animal-flowers are climbing the scaffolding –
night's instant creatures,
the neon monsters.

My heart sees its fate crucified on the sky –
a twinkling map of neon,
a huge technicolour brain,
Hungary.

Its villages, its towns,
brain cells, needles of light,
electric rivers of blue veins,
convolutions of land and brain.

I'M LOSING MY MIND!

On the third day it is hardest, on the third.

No time for cursing.
No time for crying.

But the rain is flowering a roof,
patches of wall, a hint of sky where
a tiny spider of light hangs in its web of light.
And through the dripping light-cells crawls
the mimosa leaf of advertisements,
opening, twirling, closing
like a sea-anemone's head…
slowly it sways,
feeling its way.

HELP ME SOMEONE!

But through the dripping rain-
ferns, monsters are crawling...
nylon, plastic and rubber
skins, hiss
and crackle and shine in the light as they move.

Women in lizard skins.
Men in snake skins.

They hunger.
And they thirst.

A bestiary
of red, blue, green and yellow faces.

Who knows me standing here in the cold?
Who will accept my gift of flowers?
Who are my friends? Where have they gone?
My voice is a shout in a dream.

I search the rain,
looking for you.
A blue voice calling you, calling you.

From the red, yellow and green
scribbles of light,
night sketches a shape in the rain –
a giant beer mug.
It has just a minute to live.

The amber beer sparkles like fire.
Neon lather slops over the rim
vomiting, dribbling yellow stains
of frothing electricity into the rain.

Where am I going?
What song am I singing?

"Save me, O Lord, from all evil"

On the third day it is hardest, on the third.

What am I doing here?
Where else is there?

I flounder around in the swill of neon beer.
But I feel like a child wanting to scream,
to be given something … and how the world would laugh!
O Hungary I'd climb the neon veins of your body and skull,
I'd sprawl on your neon brain
so the world could see in radiance through my ribs
my beating heart's blister,
your own heart.

No, it is not permitted.

On the third day it is hardest, on the third.

No time for cursing,
no time for weeping.
In this wilderness of rainbow and rain
I hear my grandmother's voice again –
"Save me, Lord, from the unicorn, the four-breasted bird

Save me, Lord, from the mangy ram and the whinnying flower
Save me, Lord, from the barking toad and the hooved angel
Save me O Lord, save me from all evil"

But who's there? Who am I talking to?
Who can save himself with a song?
I denied God. I laughed him away.
I flicked his balls with thorns and ran like a street-boy.
I've blown my tiny flame
to a tree of fire, ten miles high –
and the scorched insects fall like ash from the sky.
Red, blue, green,
I wear as my laurels this neon wreath,
I drown in the purple beard of a neon man
whose tentacles lick through my skull to devour the brain.

Only you can save me, you.

On the third day it is hardest, on the third.

What do I want?
What did I ever want?
I dug myself into your heart
like a soldier, numbed by the shells,
deeper and deeper into the mud of your heart
under the grinning jack o' lantern
skulls, and the shrapnel leafing like trees
all around me ... flies dabbing the blood
from the rags and swaying vines of flesh and veins
and rainbow lids and eyes twitching like flowers.

I lie curled
like a question, an embryo,

in the drumming jungle of your blood.
Your ribs sway softly like a crib,
but your heavy heartbeat shakes me,
the pulse and clutch of your entrails shakes me.
I hear the cauldron of your liver,
the sweat of your kidneys dripping phosphor;
my eye is the risen moon in your night,
its tentacles probing
for dawn in the dark of your body.
You are the depths of space and ocean to me.

I'm alone.

You are with me.

Red, blue, yellow, green…
still the rain is falling.
The sea is swirling full of phosphorous eyes.
The sea's brain, Hungary,
is a neon medusa drifting above me,
and our world, an anemone lost in the chaos of space
swims round and round in a gulf of the Milky Way.

Larva,
I know you'll shed your skin.
Your gift is flight. You will begin
stretching your frail new amber wings,
unfurling them from their glues of birth,
and their fibres will dry in the warm wind
as the wings flutter, fanning free of the blue slime –
and the womb of time will close behind
you. I know, because our fates are the same.

I'm alone.
I bow my rainsoaked head.

On the third day it is hardest, on the third.
It is Thursday evening,
no time for cursing,
no time for weeping.

Hell-bent on life, like a sponge, I head for home
in the red, green and blue rain: in the age of socialism.

About the Translator

David Wevill was born a Canadian in Yokohama, Japan, where his family had been living for two generations, in 1935. The family left for Canada before the outbreak of World War II. Wevill grew up in Canada and moved to England during the 1950s, read History and English at Caius College, Cambridge, and gained a reputation as a leading young poet in the 1960s. He lived in London, where he was associated with The Group, a gathering of young poets who met frequently to discuss their work. He moved to Texas in the late 1960s, where he co-edited *Delos: A Journal on and of Translation* and taught at the University of Texas at Austin until his retirement. His poetry was first showcased in the Penguin Modern Poets series and has since been awarded with an Arts Council Book Prize, the Richard Hillary Prize, two Arts Council Poetry Bursaries, an E.C. Gregory Trust Award, and a Guggenheim Fellowship. His work has appeared in numerous publications, including *The New York Times, The New Yorker, Poetry* (Chicago), *Harper's, The Listener, The Observer, The Spectator,* and on the BBC. In 2022 his *Collected Poems* were published by Shearsman Books in two volumes, along with a volume of his *Translations* and a collection of short prose, *Casual Ties*. David Wevill lives in Austin, Texas.

Lightning Source UK Ltd.
Milton Keynes UK
UKHW011020150822
407320UK00001B/94